stains

early poems
by Lori A. May

Also from Lori A. May

poetry chapbooks

naked
de(con)struction
cross my heart

novels

The Profiler
Moving Target

stains

early poems by

Lori A. May

L A May

Lisa —

It's so great to see you again and again and again... because this city has it all!

Keep at it

L A May

— Scarab Club '10

Bohemian Steel Press

National Library of Canada Cataloguing
in Publication Data

May, Lori A. —
stains

ISBN 978-0-9735824-0-6

I. Title

Printed and bound in the United States of America.
Bohemian Steel Press
Editor: Sandra DeSalvo
Photo Credits: "stained series" by Lori A. May

Literary Representation for Lori A. May:
Jay Poynor
The Poynor Group
13454 Yorktown Drive
Bowie MD 20715-1466

Information and media requests:
www.loriamay.com

Dedicated to C, Z, and P.

contents

grass

portrait

ribbons choke
my throat
sucking me into
pink taffeta

polished shoes
reflecting up my skirt

stockings laced
with innocent flowers
halting personality
with itchy fabric

portrait preparation
complete misrepresentation

smile wide
teeth discreet
knees together
mask reality

fingers interlaced
head tilted please

chin up
stomach in
eyes wide and
sincere

toes crammed into
second-hand shoes

patent leather
shines on
for decades
still good this year

crossed ankles
confine movement

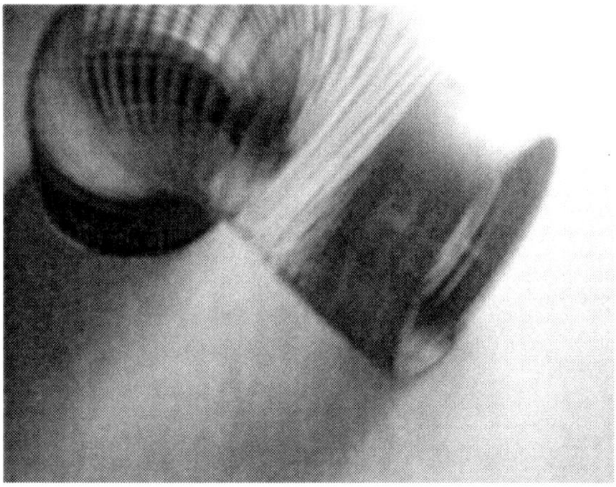

brat

my tongue
stuck out
in retaliation
defiant of her

waiting for reaction
determined on last word rights

air sucking dry
youthful fear
swallowed by spankings
raged tantrum near

stuck further in anger
pay attention to me

father noticed
and called me near
scorned matter of
disrespect made clear

wet in mouth
my tongue rests silent

bitter
and afraid
determined
to push free

summer

summer sands sweeping
across the winter of my skin
sweet tangy lemon
quenching my hot mouth
sunshine drips
and drenches my body
while lips bake
in the waves
the long awaited days
of haze and heat
have finally arrived
no longer am I a hermit
in my cave
tossed mittens and wools
socks lost and arms bared
I whisper lullabies and
chant and thank
the sky for smiling

1979

plastic covered upholstery
controls movements
as tornados swirl
and circle our home

cat under couch
ice cream melting
cone swollen
and distasteful

radio waves reaching
weather man preaching
sparks fly
aged flare no comfort

rocks pound glass
motionless breath
tension from
squished fingertips

black sheet of judgement
swallows swing sets
hopscotch bruised
and regurgitated

mailbox set free
bellyache heats
plastic melting skin
puppies bleed

coffee

mustang

he kissed me
on the hood
of his mustang
jeans against candy apple red

the kinks
rocked hard
while he sucked my youth
through parted lips

smudged fingerprints
evaporated
against freshly polished
metal

one hand
cradled my neck
the other
pulling me closer

knees parted
to close the space
he moved into me
vacuumed as guitars sang

he kissed me
on the hood
of his mustang
my sneaker scuffing the bumper

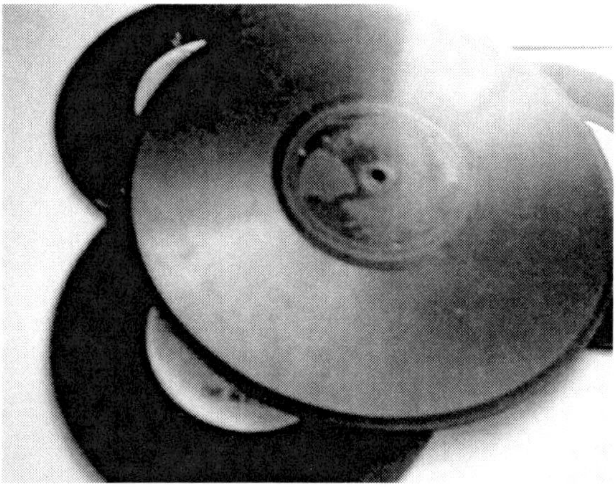

kiss

like liquid
you drip kisses over me

nectar slips
between your lips

flowing in pause

like liquid
your fingers dust against me

stirring breath
upon my neck

shivers sprinkle quietly

sleep

I wanna sleep
            with you
I said sleep
I want to
            snooze and
            lie in a heap
            of flannel and
fresh cotton
and turn the
                        clock around
            and squish
my squishy pillow
            and roll over
            and say
hi
            I want to
            shriek
when I feel
cold   toes
and warm them
with laughter
I want to hear
snoring and know
that someone is
            sleeping at ease
I want to wake up
            freezing
because you've got
all the covers
            and smile

cuz you've got
all the covers
I want to watch
you while
you dream of
being a big rock star
with fans so
excited
I want to hear the
rain fall outside
the window
and hear you say
'let's not get up today'
I want to sleep with you
so I can get some rest

cream

Cream is the colour
When our skin is naked and in love
It doesn't lie or hide behind distraction
Simply causes reaction
And fades and rises with you and I

Black is the truth
When your irises shine
Too much for my soul to take
Blinded

Blush is the fantasy
Where we meet and mingle
Not knowing what day it is
Not caring what world this is

Clear is the vision
I have when I'm with you
No pretension or indecision

Just momentary extended repetition
Never enough seconds in the split

Blue is the colour
Of the veins under your skin
A river I chase every moment
Trying to dig deeper
And discover your ocean

Cream is the colour
Bruised and blushed
Like petals extended
Delicate. Fearless. Exposed.

caramel

your breath drips
like melted caramel

sweet
sticky

bittersweet cider of your tongue
flicking
crispy
with bite

cookie crumble
of your touch
chips fall
against my cheek

buttercup caresses
syrups rolling over me

ink

chapters

crackling flames
backdrop to night's fall
lights dim and flicker

toes curled into comfort
pages dusty with age

ribbons trace
passages
lazy Sunday haze

stained with time

words roll off the tongue
crackling flames
squinting eyes

dreams await

knock

there was love for a moment
when I didn't think about it

it came to say hello

a stranger
I did not open the door
but peeped through the hole

unsure what to say
deadbolt in my way

stepped silently away
hoping it would not notice

quiet now
until footsteps begin
breathing still
then loud

the apartment

Your apartment
Down the hall
Down the stairs

Morning coffees
And afternoon teas
Naps with ease

Flipping pages of
Favourite prose
Bookmarked for a moment

After dinner sessions
Of discussion and bewilderment
Sharing separate togetherness

Dustcovers and ink
Pages of history
Sound recordings connecting the floors

Records skipping
Clocks unplugged
Down the stairs I wander

Unlocked doors
Opened arms
Together with ease

Best of both worlds
Notes as reminders
Of what to share over brunch

Kisses extended
Breaking to inspire
Muses neighboured peacefully

Two-foot radius
Boundaries respected
Blurred in union

Mid-evening cocktails
Laughter from above
Secret hideaways

Smell the age of inspiration
Share the passion of time
Listen to a.m. radio

Sketches complete
Passages fully expressed
You come up to my apartment

# of wips and want

Blank pages spread before me
Like legs, limber and longing
Looking for identity.

Painted words lick up the white
Resting in their newfound home.

You are a work in progress.

Paris, just there

There is laughter beneath these sheets.

December slush puddles around your name
Swooping up measures of summered pleasures,
killing time with freedom and frivolity.

You gush forth with brilliance
Shining like the new moon over oceans,
Stirring quakes and rupturing sweet silence.

Come to me now
With winds dancing merrily,
Carrying your why and how,
Bringing all measures of being through lightness.

Purposeful and pleasantly,
Dance through the streets
And cheer against crowds
Disturbed by holiday bliss.

Where fogs find nestled intentions,
Comfort against glass,
Speak in poetics and sonnets
rhyming rhythms with me.

Pretend Paris is just there
On the other side of the street.
Swim across the channel,
or Thames as it may be,
and push through the laughter,

clinging ever so gently to snow-capped curbs
to lead you
through sheets and gusts and puddles of peace,
and sing lullabies in languages we wish we could speak.

salt

minute

she lets him believe
not knowing how else to say
the disturbing thoughts

he smiles and lights up
thinking he has it made
she can't disagree

it scares her
when she doesn't pay attention
feels it slipping away

in front of her
she doesn't realize
now is never coming back

smart girls

smart girls don't think
she says
just keep your thoughts to yourself

smart girls don't talk
she says
that mouth of yours can be big trouble

they don't want little girls
telling them what to do she says
they want to feel as though
they are kings

even the she-kings she says
who protect their own
by putting you into place

smart girls don't do that
she says
for they are bound to misunderstand

smart girls don't think
she says
as they should know better than that

smart girls don't try
to get anywhere with them
she says

there's no room for your kind
in their kingdom of sin

smart girls don't talk
she says
and waste their words on worms

# of blood and wine

Upon your departure, melancholy arrives
in a drunken unease,
from wine I did not partake.

Someday I wish to know you
and understand your superficial presentation.
There is personality under that skin,
years of experience lending to your demeanour.

I wonder if you think at night,
when the walls contain only you,
of truth and honesty and all contradictions;
If you ponder your state
and create purposeful delusions.

Once when no one was looking
you spoke to me with soft skin,
and for a moment
I wanted to drink your blood
while it was briefly untainted.

Callused friend, I know your intent.

You mean well and aim to please
and I think
that's precisely the dilemma at hand.

Someday I wish to know you,
see beyond the shell
of flesh which protects you,

so your departure leaves
only trails of reality,
too sad to keep cover.

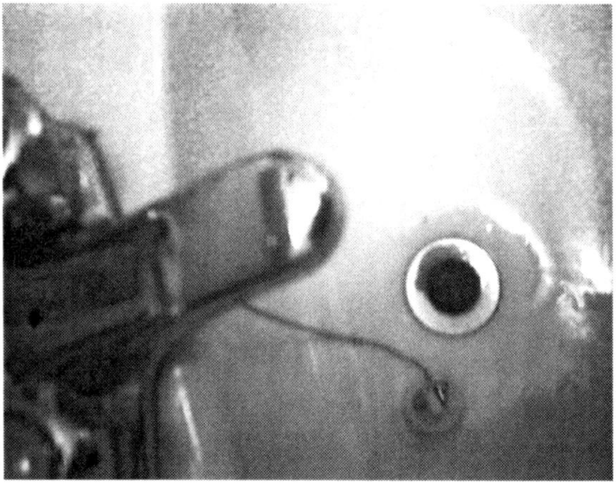

choice

he remembers who he was going to be
and it hurts his tomorrow
pains his past
reminds him of a youth
that barely did breathe

there was once a moment
he knew would come free
where he could become
the man he would be

trading
settling
compromising

all in good fun
it's the right thing to do
his head and heart agreed

but years have come
years have passed
and all that remains
is the reflection

broken
shattered
stunted

the memory remains the memory

smoke

u.04.01

What happens
when the mice
are all
gone?

u.04.03

the only reason
for truth
is to permit
judgement

u.04.07

the lack
of expectation

does not
guarantee
protection from

disappointment

u.99.07

whisper
          touch
kiss

whisper touch   kiss

          whisper
touch
kiss

a whispering touch kisses me

u.04.05

I am wine
fluid and bold
smooth like glass

shattered mosaic

blood

war

you deny
confrontation
and ignore
response

act in silence
to mask
insecurity

cry out at war
yet drop atoms

against rabbits
crying

screeching innocence
challenged questions

trapped
in paper bags

soiled sheets
and ripped fingernails

gunshots
mask ignorance
merry-go-round
hides graves

Dear

shoot it
he begged of
his ten year old son

send metal
and pain
to beat the Dear

stand tall
and demand
it falls to its grave

shoot it
you are no coward
son of mine

take aim
and courage
to deafen the forest

shoot it
and show them
who is in charge

powered with adrenaline
to disguise
your tears

shoot it
and tower above
its weeping eyes

the food chain
will thank you
for claiming your right

shoot it
and show the world
you are guilt free

because you can
is the reason
no room for uncertainty

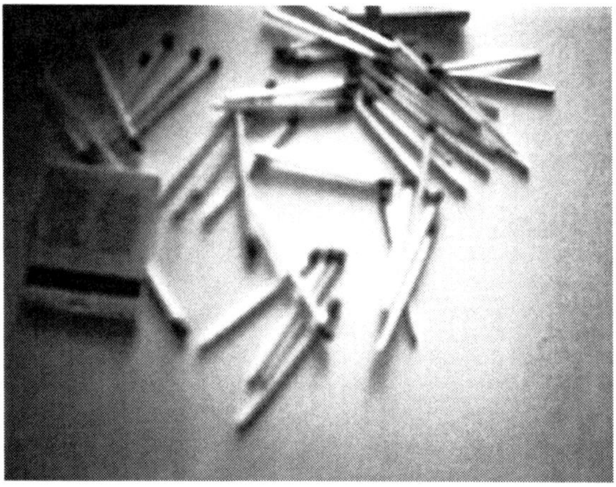

third

Go ahead
And send them
Your basket of fruit
And first aid kits

Go ahead
And say prayers
Your preaching ways
Seep through neon lights

You cry out
In anger
And passionate words

Lulling them
Protecting them

Yet they are your prey

Go ahead
And build schools
Wrap knowledge
With insight

Go ahead
And harvest crops
Shaking their hands
In commerce

You smile and wave
For the camera today

Yet tomorrow strike matches

Go ahead
And give scholarships
To deserving children
Of god

Go ahead
And send money
Before taxing
Their wheat and water

You cry out
In response
Your name has been called

Killing their attempts
At controlling their fate

Yet shaking hands with the devil

Go ahead
And provide for them
Technology
And supplies

Go ahead
And employ them
Wrapped silently
Around your thumb

You pay them
To create
That which will kill them

Yet apply make-up to look good on film

Go ahead
And bless babies
Who have no
Right to vote

Go ahead
And tax people
For breathing
Public air

You scar them
With toxins
And pollute their water

Yet colour it beautiful

Go ahead
And make bombs
From dust and
Raised dollars

Go ahead
And remove them
From a quiet life
Of happiness

You own them
For a penny
Shiny with bloodshed

Yet ask for forgiveness in mourning

sweat

u.05.20

I eat cottage cheese
Straight from the plastic tub,
Spoon dipped in the treasure chest
Pulling pieces together randomly.

Sometimes I single out
A cold nub and exclude it,
Letting its flesh become bare
And warm against my tongue.

As I squish its being flat,
I think of you
And how your fingers taste at night.

DNA

I want to find the one place
No one else has touched you

One place no one has left prints
Or memories

It is waiting
Brewing and breathing
Quietly seeking attention
From a secret hunter

One who is hungry
Thirsty for life yet unborn

I want to find the one place
No one else has punctured

One place
I can call my own

Could be the obvious
The overlooked
Underdog

It sits
Humbly
Obedient
Waiting its turn

For someone detailed
And precise
To call on it
And let it sing

I want to find the one place
Where I can leave my prints
The one place
Where only I have touched you

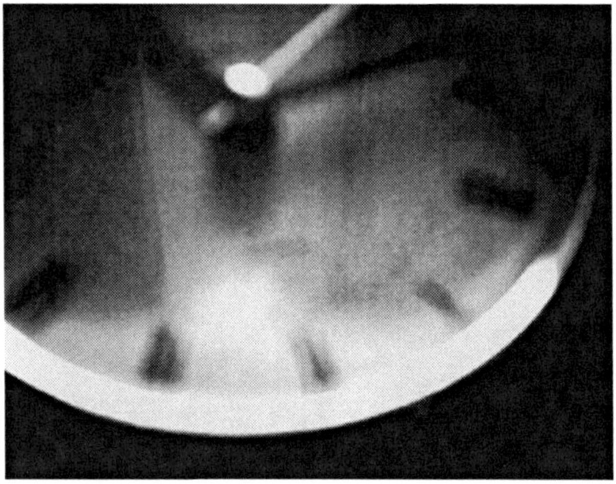

the beach

Let's pretend this is Love Story
or Grease,
but perhaps we should pinkie swear off
tragic moments and endings.

We can race through the water's edge
chasing winter away with the June love bug,
crashing down into the moist mattress of nature.

Pull a twig from my hair,
brush the salt from my skin
and lick up midnight along my spine.

Lapping applause from the lake
will lull us into bliss,
accentuating our first summer kiss.

Blow a sweet breeze
into the dimple of my ear,
let me hear
how much you want me to mix up the dirt.

Later we can watch the sky
and trace the starlit paths
along our naked backs,
comparing constellations.

When you're hungry
I'll bring you malted vinegar fries
and we'll squish them one by one
against our laughter.

Before falling asleep in the sandwich
of earth and sky, you say
we'll never leave here,
because that's when tragedy strikes
and the water separates from the sand.

morning

bodies disconnected
side by side in distance
deceived identities
flashbacks reunited

brushed teeth and coffee stains
rumpled sheets
quiet pale noise
to speak

casual conversation
denial and frustration
no inspection for fear
shadows drift along drapery

bones crack against stretches
sunbeams taunt misdirection
distance slipping loose hairs
and blurred vision

burnt toast snapping hard
against clanking sips
breaking the tension
causing attention

self-defeat and triumph
wrapped and intertwined
newspapers blotting
fingerprints remain and disguise

grandfather clock ticks
scratches underneath fingertips
distance slowing
and air swallows time

horns honking
doors creak with steps
intent on disappearing
scuffed floors slightly wet

acknowledgements

Thank you to the following publications where some of the poems in this collection appear or are forthcoming.

Applecart Magazine
"cream"
"summer"

The Claremont Review
"sleep"

The Coffee Press Journal
"caramel"
"minute"
"summer"

The Poetry of Food CFP Anthology
"caramel"

The Poetry of Love CFP Anthology
"Paris, just there"

Red Fez Publications
"cream"
"DNA"

Van Gogh's Ear, Volume 5
"of blood and wine"

Zygote
"sleep"

a note on stains, *from the author*

stains has an original copyright of 2004. The poems presented herein represent a selection of my early works, some poems dating back more than a decade. Though the project was set aside for several years, it is a project I am pleased to share with readers. My style and voice has evolved during my development as a poet and writer, but I have always believed there is value in remembering where we start out. I hope you enjoy this modest early collection. Thank you.

about the author

Lori A. May is a poet, novelist, and freelance writer whose work has appeared in publications such as *The Writer, Two Review, Tipton Poetry Journal*, and anthologies such as *Van Gogh's Ear*. She is the Founding Editor of *The Ambassador Poetry Project* and *The Western Literary Review*, a college writing instructor, and an advocate for emerging authors and artists. She has an admitted addiction to caffeine.

A native of southwestern Ontario, Lori now resides on the Michigan shoreline.

For more information, visit her online:
www.loriamay.com

Printed in the United States
153486LV00002B/1/P

9 780973 582406